CHILDREN
OF BLESSING
EMPOWERING

Quinceañero Quinceañera

I0459453

Copyright © 2025 by Carl Beard

All rights reserved.
No part of this publication may be reproduced in any form,
by photostat, microfilm, xerography, or any other means, or
incorporated into any information retrieval system, electronic or
mechanical, without the written permission of the copyright writer.

All inquiries should be addressed to:

Book Domain LLC.
543 E Louise Dr Phoenix, Az 85050

Ordering Information:
Amount Deals. Special rebates are accessible on the amount bought
by corporations, associations, and others. For points of interest,
contact the distributor at the address above.

Printed in the United States of America.

ISBN-13   Paperback   978-1-967903-70-2
           eBook   978-1-967903-71-9

Library of Congress Control Number: 2025916722

CHILDREN
OF BLESSING
EMPOWERING

Quinceañero Quinceañera

CARL BEARD

BOOK DOMAIN LLC

ACKNOWLEDGMENTS

This book would not be possible without God's love And the wisdom of the Holy Spirit. I would like to thank the following people for their contributions to this book:

The Israeli people for safeguarding the Torah.

The Jewish community for their
parental blessings heritage.
Pastor John Kilpatrick for his father's heart
and rich heritage of blessing stories.
Pastor Jack Hayford, Craig Hill, and Focus
on the Family for their ground breaking
work in blessing our children.
My pastor, Steve Dittmar, for his vision
and support over the last 25 years.
All of you who have proofread the
many manuscripts of this book.

Special thanks to Marty Lythgoe for his loving wisdom and helpful hints along the way.

To my wife Vickie.
During our fourty one years of marriage you have been a great life partner, fabulous editor and master teacher.

DEDICATED TO THE MEMORY OF
LYLE BEARD
A GRANDFATHER WHO PLANTED SEEDS OF
SUCCESS IN ME—AT AN EARLY AGE

INTRODUCTION

A man puts a message in a bottle and
hopes someone will find him.

A father puts a message in his children
and hopes they will find God.

Holy Spirit – 2006

God wants to mentor, protect and empower your
children. We release God to do this by blessing our
children. As spiritual beings our children need to be
informed, educated and empowered to succeed in life.
I know that every parent wants their child to succeed.
This book informs, educates and empowers
every parent to do the following for their child.
- Plant seeds of success in their heart.
- Water the tender heart of their child.
- See their child transformed into a young adult

fully equipped to meet life's challenges.

I promise you, no, God guarantees it by His very own Word.

"And all your (spiritual) children shall be disciples taught by the LORD (and obedient to His will) and great shall be the peace and undisturbed composure of your children."

Isaiah 54:13 (Amplified Bible)

Enjoy the thrilling and rewarding journey of blessing your children into success.

Carl A. Beard

CONTENTS

BLESSING FOUNDATIONS

All over the world and from the beginning of time parents have wanted a good future for their children. In today's societies it seems that parents are desperate to find the formula that will guarantee their children's success. If it's not soccer, karate, or music lessons – you name it and parents have tried it. Children of Blessing was written to transfer the keys of success from parents to their children.

As physical, emotional and spiritual beings our children need to be informed, educated and empowered to succeed in life. I know that if you are reading this book you want the best for your child.

As a father I thought, "Hey, I love my kids! I am a hard working dad, who brings home a paycheck, and provides for his family. What more do they want from me? Something only I can give." None of my relatives can do it. Not even God can do this. Wait a minute, not even God? That is right. He set it up that way. As men we sometimes marvel at how our wives have that sixth sense. They pick up on things or just know what to do in a situation with the children. Men also have this gift operating in them. It's the "Dad Blessing Gift." You don't have to train for it. It comes naturally.

Either parent can give the blessing. It is simple and fun to apply these powerful principles. Do you have to do it all the time? No. Do you have to teach your kids how to do it? No. They learn by your example.

BLESSING FOUNDATIONS

Then why do I do it ? Because in blessing your children, activating a gift that God placed in you when He created the world. If you don't release the gift you may not like how your children may turn out.

When you release a blessing you are literally fallowing in God's footstep[s. Genesis 1:28 says, Then God blessed them and God said to them," Be fruitful and multiply, fill the earth and subdue (rule) it". Like God, you are passing the blessing down through the generations.

You frame your child's life through speaking the blessings God has placed in the family line of mankind.

Proverbs 18:21 says it best. "Death and life (blessings) are in the power of (your) tongue and they that love it shall eat the fruit of it." Here is the first clue to releasing a blessing. You have a choice of speaking death or life into your child's life. So choose to speak life to them.

We are going to look at the dynamic of a blessing as described in the manufacture's handbook (the Bible). We will look in on a typical family found in Genesis chapter 27. Father Abraham had blessed his son Isaac and now Isaac was going to bless who he thought was his oldest son Esau.

BLESSING FOUNDATIONS

Notice what Isaac says to his son Jacob as he blesses him.

"May God give you the dew of heaven.

Of the fatness of the earth and plenty of grain and wine. Let peoples serve you and nations bow down to you. Be master over your brethren and let your mother's sons bow down to you. Cursed be everyone who curses you and blessed be those that bless you."

Genesis 27: 27-29

Does this blessing talk about multiplication?

Yes it does.

Does this blessing talk about leadership?

Yes it does.

Does this blessing frame this child's life?

Yes it does.

What was the result of Isaac's blessing over his son?

Jacob became the father of the twelve tribes of Israel.

He became a very wealthy man who left a legacy to his descendants. You may notice that this is consistent with God's blessing in Genesis 1:28.

Now let's look at Esau's point of view.

Why is Esau upset when he does not get his blessing?

You see, the family authority was tied to the blessing of the first born. Genesis 27:29

BLESSING FOUNDATIONS

Esau begs his father to give him some kind of blessing. In his culture Isaac could not rescind the blessing he just gave to Jacob. Esau ends up getting the crumbs of a blessing.

All of us want to receive a blessing, especially from our fathers. There is good news for us today. We can bless each one of our children with a full blessing, no matter the order they were born.

Let us try Issac's blessing in today's language:

Son or Daughter you will always be in good health and have enough for every need and desire.

You will succeed in every job you do.

You will always have favor with everyone you work with.

Wherever you go, people will go out of their way to help you.

You will be a leader and not a follower.
God will always show you the right way to go.

You will have peace like a royal prince / princess because you know God is with you.

Can you see how your words are framing your child's success in life.

BLESSING FOUNDATIONS

Now some of us might also be thinking, "Wait a minute! Just saying nice things about my kids went out when they turned two. You need to control kids or they will control you."

Consistently blessing your children, no matter what they are doing or saying, plants a seed in their heart (or spirit). Here is what God's word says: "Train up a child in the way they should go and when they grow older they shall not turn from it." Proverbs 22:6 When you train a vine you use a rod to direct and support the vine's growth. When you speak words of blessing you create the same effect. You provide direction and support for the growth of your child. These blessings act as roots that anchor your child's life. How deep will these roots go? Only time and circumstance will tell.

I hope this helps to lay a foundation of blessing. You speak to your children in a normal loving way and God takes care of the rest. It is easy and it is very powerful.

THE POWER OF WORDS

God's words are truth and they are life. We will uncover the power of these words and your words as we unlock the truth in His words.

Truth is defined by Webster's Dictionary as:
Accordance with knowledge fact or actuality. The real state of affairs. Jesus said," And you shall know the truth and the truth shall make you free."

John 8:32

It is important that we as parents and children have an accurate view of the blessing. There are many people groups and religions that practice some type of coming of age ceremony. I am not saying they are all bad, some of them would frighten anybody.

Let's look into what the manufacturers handbook (The Bible) has to say about it God has given parents the choice to bless children, no mater what stupid things their child does. you may be able to think about a situation where you chose to say something positive instead of something negative.

Proverb 18:21 says,"Death and life are in the power of the tongue and they that love it shall eat the fruit of it."

THE POWER OF WORDS

As you can see, we all have a choice. I am not encouraging you to create a false reality. I am encouraging you to look for the good, or God's word in every situation. Did you notice that Isaac did not finish with "Amen", Or "Thus sayeth the Lord"?

He spoke from his heart. He spoke good things. He empowered his son to prosper. Consistency is the key here.

Human beings were made to receive blessings throughout their lives. It is interesting to note that God never considers Himself a grandfather but a father. There is a one to one relationship between each human being in this world and their creator. We don't have to make a big production out of it. That should take all the pressure off getting it right. It does for me.

There is a place for a prophetic word or even a prayer over a child. When it comes to blessing, we can just say it without having to end it with and "Amen", or a "Thus says the Lord". How about, "I love you".

PLANTING SEEDS OF SUCEESS

When I asked God for direction, in explaining the truth behind this blessing process, I was directed to the fallowing scripture.

"But when the sun was up it was scorched, and because it had no root it withered away."

Mark 4:6

The sixth verse of Mark chapter four reveals what happened to a seed that was sown on good ground. The sun, like circumstances, was beating down on the seed. You know like all those challenges that you and your child face every day.

The sun, like those challenges, shines all the time. It is no respecter of persons. Life is always in your face, no matter your age.

The word "scorched" means that when great heat is applied to the outside of paper or a plant it turns color. (Webster Dictionary)

Just because we get scorched does not mean we automatically give up and die. It means that we may turn a different color, like when you are embarrassed or mad. Remember to keep on blessing your child, even when you are scorched.

After meditating on this scripture for a while the Holy Spirit gave me a clue. No Seed – No Root.

PLANTING SEEDS
OF SUCCESS

Or we might say it this way. No Blessing – No Future. But wait a minute. The Sower sowed the seed on good ground. Metaphorically, the seeds can be our parental blessings. Jesus later explained the Word of God is a seed.

Then it came to me. Just because we create controlled environments for our children, does not guarantee that the seed of our blessing grows.

Paul the apostle wrote: "Faith comes by hearing and hearing by the word of God". Romans 4:17 We want to adopt this spiritual law to our blessing situation. We can say our children's faith in their blessing to succeed in life comes from hearing our blessings on a continual basis.

So how do our blessings grow up with strong roots? I am glad you asked. The answer is water and tend your seeds continually. As fathers we have the privilege of preparing the ground with love so our seeds of blessing have a good environment. We can bless them early and often. Do not wait until they graduate college, high school, junior high or even the first grade to start blessing. You start the moment you see them all bundled up in the hospital nursery.

PLANTING SEEDS
OF SUCCESS

Some of you got a head start, by blessing your children in the womb. Now that is a proactive blessing. But what happened to the root?

The tongue plants seeds of blessings in your child's heart. the heart stores and incubates those blessings. No blessings in the heart (or spirit) and you probably won't get a root to withstand the scorching. It is guaranteed the scorching will come. It is all part of life.

So how do we protect our investment ?
A wise man once said. " Keep (or protect) your heart with all diligence. For out of it spring the issues of life." Proverbs 4:23

That is right ! ALL your words of blessing or cursing are being stored up in your child's heart. So keep those blessings coming.

Here is an example we can all relate to:

We can build a green house, put in all the sprinkler systems, stock up the plant food and fill the plant beds with dirt. This does not guarantee growth. I still need to plant the seed, watch it and nurture it. WE can create a healthy environment on all levels, but without a blessing it is just a healthy environment. Don't get me wrong environments are very powerful factors in people's lives. Think about this-—Blessings lead to growth and growth leads to endurance and endurance produces much good fruit.

PLANTING SEEDS
OF SUCCESS

Here is a great resource that will help in the nurturing process. "Bar Barakah A Parent's Guide to a Christian Bar Mitzvah", by Craig Hill No, it is not an incantation, **but** the Hebrew word for the blessing. Craig Hill is **the founder of Family Foundations Ministries. He is a respected author, lecturer and a good friend of mine. After helping lots of families with all kinds of problems, folks asked Craig if he would write down all those words of wisdom, and he has. This is a great resource in dealing with teenagers.**

You might be thinking, "My kids are doing fine, they don't need any extra blessings". Well listen to this: Researchers have found an interesting correlation between the inmates in prison and the lack of blessings from their FATHERS. No blessing was

found in their testimonies. I think you are getting the picture by now. Before we move on, we have another resource for you. Senior Pastor Jack Hayford of Church on the Way – Van Nuys, California has written another wonderful reference book," The Blessing". It has all kinds of good examples on blessing your child. I would recommend this book for every father's library.

What have we discovered so far? When God puts a spiritual law to work, He first describes it in His handbook, (The Bible). You can then count on it working every time you apply it.

1. Focus on the Family "Fathers and their Child's Behavior

TURNING HEARTS RELEASING BLESSINGS

God's plan is to turn the hearts of the fathers to the children and the hearts of the children to the fathers. NO wonder evil forces have been working overtime to destroy the family unit, all around the world. God is very serious about this.

"And he will turn(God's prophetic voice)
The hearts of the fathers to the children…
And the heart of the children to their fathers.
Lest I come and strike the earth with a curse."

Malachi 4:6

When you bless your child With word's of blessing your child's heart is turned to you and to God's nurturing touch. He now has permission to reveal his blessing to your child. With attention like this your blessings have a chance to grow roots that build a strong foundation for your child's success in life. So you can see that a father's consistent blessing is instrumental to framing and empowering your child's transition into their inheritance of blessings. Faith in your blessings comes from hearing and hearing your blessings. Our children must continually hear our words of blessing. Remember the secret to Jacob's success was Isaac's words of blessing. In our blessing services we encourage the birth father to participate. Yes even if the mom has raised the child

TURNING HEARTS
RELEASING BLESSINGS

We also invite older men to participate in place of that missing dad. But it is OKAY for moms to stand in place of dads. God's grace is big enough for that. If Mary, the mother of Jesus, had shown up at the temple without Joseph, the priests would have honored the blessing ceremony.

Pastor John Kilpatrick, (Brownsville Revival), says, "Blessings are not a prayer, they are not a prophetic word", and they obviously are not an incantation. So what is a blessing? (It should be noted that a blessing could turn out to be a prophetic statement.) Moms and dads remember, God's grace is big enough to allow both of you to bless your children. In fact, every member of the family should help to support your child's blessings. Blessing should never be a ritual, it should be natural.

It should be something all parents do because it's a gift inside of them. I have good news. Blessing your child does not have to be complex or technical. But it does require a systematic approach. What seems to look complex and technical are all the curves life throws at us. Remember, the heat of the sun shines on us all.

In life, we all get chances to give and receive blessings. It all starts at birth with baby dedications. You may sprinkle them, pray over them or hold them up buck naked to the Lord. God does not seem to frown on any of these practices.

TWO FAMILIES AND THE BLESSING

Well its time to tell you the story behind this book and how our family has traveled down the road of blessings.

About 15 years ago my Pastor, Steve Dittmar, (Jubilee Church-Camarillo, CA,) shared his blessing dream with the congregation. It was simple but very powerful. the dream was to have a family of four generations that where Christians. Most families have a generation or two before somebody gets off the blessing path. He wanted to make sure his children and their children had a sure foundation and transition into their blessings from God. My wife Vickie and I took up the dream as a challenge for our family. As a school teacher Vickie is a researcher and before long she had me reading all kinds of Jewish literature on Bar and Bat Mitzvahs. One celebration is for boys the other for girls. We took the challenge seriously. We wanted four generations of our children serving God. You noticed I did not say grandchildren. I am adopting God's technique of having a one on one relationship with all my descendents.

Many people today think that their children will never amount to anything. this comes from a philosophy that says "Its hopeless, my kids will never turn out right. Our family has a long line of unsuccessful people in it." I have good news for you.

TWO FAMILIES AND THE BLESSING

That is a plain, bold face lie that will never stand up to God's Love and His word. Maybe I should give you a snapshot of our family history as an example. I come from a broken home. My stepfather was abusive and I never really knew my real father. He left us when I was five. I was placed in an orphanage in Mexico City where I waited for my mother to bring me and my brothers up to the states. When we arrived in the states we were placed in a boy's home for a short period of time. It was there, at Sunshine Acres, that I met the Messiah and received His love into my life. My brothers and I finally came to live with our mother. Our family moved to California and within a few years my mother divorced my stepdad. She became a Jehovah's Witness and I studied under them for three years before leaving home. Not a great history for blessing.

My wife was raised in a very stable home. (She had a happy childhood and always had enough.) Her grandmother is the one who imparted to her the knowledge of God. Her parents felt that children should make the decision for themselves when they were adults. God found her right before her eighth birthday. Thank God for Vickie's grandmothers who prayed over their granddaughter!

TWO FAMILIES AND
THE BLESSING

In our earthly father's house we learn to submit to his authority. Hey, that is exactly what Jesus did when His parents came and picked Him up from the temple.

Our son Jacob had some challenges with submission at first. He rebelled and went his own way for a short time. He returned to submit to his father, and we now enjoy a mutually satisfying father/son relationship. Jacob actively seeks our counsel and the counsel of God. He now serves in the U.S. Navy. Jacob has learned his lessons of service and now it is his way of life.

We also decided to give each one of our children a ring as a symbol of their wholeness and virginity. This was a tangible symbol of passing from one place in life to another. It was a reminder of their wholeness—

spiritually, physically and mentally. We had a great party and many guests decided that they too would like to have an event like this. Just recently, we had one of those families celebrate their son's coming of age in a very distinct manner. More on that shortly. For the event, we purchased new clothes for our children. You might remember Joseph got a coat of many colors that marked him for the family line of blessing. All these things act to reinforce your blessings. They mark your children for transition into a successful life.

Our oldest daughter, Sheralee, was given the charge to maintain her purity until marriage. My wife and I prayed over her and our pastor blessed her. Some of

UNTIL DEATH DO US PART

Recently Pastor John Kilpatrick visited our church and shared a wedding blessing story with our congregation. He had started having the parents of the bride and Groom, give a blessing at the beginning of the wedding ceremony. Our church has embraced this powerful practice.

My wife Vickie and I had the privilege of blessing both of our daughters during their marriage ceremonies. Both experiences were very powerful. We were able to release our parental blessing into the lives of our new son-in-laws as well. Vickie and I saw a dream come true with the marriage of our youngest daughter. We gave her a ring at her 13th birthday signifying her accountability as an adult and covenant with God. She stood faithful and entered into her covenant relationship with her husband with a "This is my daughter in whom I am well pleased" blessing from her dad. What a wonderful blessing time we will never forget. Now we are going to look at our second family. Remember, others are watching you bless your children and will want to emulate your actions.

ADULT BLESSING

This book would not be complete unless we talked about the adult blessing. God promises us that His mercies are new every morning. Just because you missed your Bar or Bar Mitzvah, or you were never blessed by your parents, does not mean you have missed out. There is no time limit on blessing. You can get your blessing at any time.

Can an adult go through a blessing ceremony? The answer is " yes and amen". Remember God does not have grandchildren. Everyone of us who have received Him as our Savior is His child. Thousands of adults have gone back to that point in life and filled in a giant hole. I turn to Pastor John Kilpatrick's true story to make this point. There was a young man who could not hold a job, or develop a serious relationship. But he heard the message of blessing from Pastor Kilpatrick. So the young man goes home and asks his very belligerent dad to bless him. The father complies, at first grudgingly. Then the father actually breaks down during this time of blessing. The happy ending is that this young man suddenly has the confidence to go for a job interview, and is dating a young lady. Why? Because the cursing words that his dad had originally spoken over him, were broken by the blessing. There is NO age limit. Men and women can go back and get their blessing, even if their parents have passed away. With God, all things are possible. Remember, it is never too late to celebrate a blessing. Even if you are 99 years old.

YOUR BLESSING

I bless you with good, sound health and a
prosperous mind and emotions.
I bless you with a whole and complete family.
Nothing missing and nothing broken.
I bless you with a vision to see four generations
of your family serving God.
I bless you in your traveling to and from your
home, your work and your city.
I bless you with insight to see life's pitfalls and
the wisdom to side step them altogether.
I bless you with God's goodness, mercy and
His presence every day of your life.
BE BLESSED

PREPARING FOR A BLESSING

Here are questions that will help get the ball rolling:

What gifts and natural talents has God given to me?

What is my passion in life?

(I like to travel or help people, etc.)

What words from God or others do I have in my life?

What life scriptures keep coming up in a person's life? They are either repeated or a theme is repeated. Yes even eleven year olds get and receive words about their life. Esther Ilnisky's book, "Let the Children Pray", is a must read for any one wondering what young children are capable of.

Have them write a paragraph on each area – God, Family and Community. Then take the paragraph and condense it down to two or three sentences. They could then recite this at the ceremony.

Remember regalia, or no regalia, four generations of representation or not, YOU can have a great blessing time for your child. It's a time you and your child will always remember. God's word guarantees it.

Here are a few more tips:

Start talking to your child about this transition six months to a year before the event. Make sure to get their input about the party. Try to do this in a calm and peaceful setting. This will create a real sense of expectation on everyone's part.

BLESSING SERVICE OUTLINE

- The blessing service should not exceed 40 minutes.
- Pastor or elder to give opening prayer.
- Introduction of individuals being celebrated-by parent
- Mc or coordinator will direct parents and friends to write blessings in the blessing book.
- Introductory music or Song
- Child reads life scripture
- MC, Coordinator or parent explains the child's faith project.
- Child leaves podium and walks over small bride symbolizing change.
- Closing Music or song

- MC or facilitator welcomes all to move to the celebration are for food and drinks.
- Sibling go around collecting blessings.
- Parents thank guests for coming and officially close the gathering.

CHECK LIST & JOB RESPONSIBILITIES

Parents: Sponsors of the party
Work with child to get them ready.

Party Coordinator:
Provide background support-Facility, Food, Cleanup
Intercessors
Church Staff

Family Members: Provide blessing
Siblings : Collect blessing in blessing book
Pastor: Provide spiritual covering
Photographer: Provide Photos and video as arranged for

INVITATIONS

Invitations can be simple or fancy

SON/DAUGHTER
Blessing
Service

When

Time

Where

Now we brethren, as Isaac was, are children of the Promise
Galatians 4:28

A PDF copy of the blessing
servi planner and quest singing book are
available free at www.prayertab.com

BIBLIOGRAPHY

New King James Spirit Filled Bible - Jack Hayford
-Nelson Publishing

Bar Baraka A Parents Guide to a Christian Bar mitzvah
Craig Hill—

The Blessing—Jack Hayford - Nelson Publishing

The Brownsville Revival-John Kilpatrick

Let the Children Pray-Esther ilnisky - World of Books

ABOUT THE AUTHOR

Carl A Beard: with three generations serving

After 25 years of educating, empowering and transforming men women and children in Christian Ministry, Carl has compiled many well proven strategies, and techniques that help people of all ages receive their blessing Carl is a grandfather to 13 beautiful prosperous grandchildren and 3 spectacular and successful children. He is an active road cyclist and enjoys sailing.

ORDER FORM PAGE

	QTY	PRICE	TOTAL
Children of promise book			
Children of promise CD			
1-10 books			
Total			
Please make checks payable to			
Credit card purchases can be made on the web www://pryaretab.com			

www.ingramcontent.com/pod-product-compliance
Lightning Source LLC
Chambersburg PA
CBHW061718120626
46550CB00003B/1268